GALE
CENGAGE Learning·

Short Stories for Students, Volume 8

Staff

Editorial: Ira Mark Milne, *Editor*. Tim Akers, Dave Galens, Polly Vedder, Kathleen Wilson, *Contributing Editors*. James P. Draper, *Managing Editor*.

Research: Victoria B. Cariappa, *Research Team Manager*. Cheryl Wamock, *Research Specialist*. Patricia T. Ballard, Conine A. Boland, Wendy Festerling, Tamara Nott, Tracie A. Richardson, *Research Associates*. Timothy Lehnerer, Patricia Love, *Research Assistants*.

Permissions: Maria Franklin, *Permissions Manager*. Kimberly Smilay, *Permissions Specialist*. Kelly Quin, *Permissions Associate*. Sandra K. Gore, Erin Bealmear, *Permissions Assistants*.

Production: Mary Beth Trimper, *Production Director*. Evi Seoud, *Assistant Production Manager*. Cindy Range, *Production Assistant*.

Imaging and Multimedia Content Team: Randy Bassett, *Image Database Supervisor*. Robert Duncan, Michael Logusz, *Imaging Specialists*. Pamela A. Reed, *Imaging Coordinator*.

Product Design Team: Cynthia Baldwin, *Product Design Manager*. Pamela A. E. Galbreath, *Senior Art Director*. Gary Leach, *Graphic Artist*.

coordination, expression, arrangement, and classification of information. All rights to this publication will be vigorously defended.

The Legend of Sleepy Hollow

Washington Irving

1820

Introduction

The great American short story "The Legend of Sleepy Hollow" was written while Washington Irving was living in England, and it was published in England in a volume called *The Sketch Book of Geoffrey Crayon, Gent*. The *Sketch Book* was published in installments in the United States beginning in 1819, but the section that included this story was not issued until 1820. Readers on both sides of the Atlantic Ocean thus encountered the story at approximately the same time.

"The Legend of Sleepy Hollow" takes place in Sleepy Hollow, New York, a snug rural valley near Tarrytown in the Catskill Mountains. Constructed from German tales but set in America, it is a classic tale of the conflict between city and country, and between brains and brawn. Ichabod Crane courts Katrina Van Tassel, but is frightened away by his rival, Brom Bones, masquerading as the headless horseman. The story demonstrates the two qualities for which Irving is best known: his humor, and his ability to create vivid descriptive imagery.

Readers immediately took to "The Legend of Sleepy Hollow" and another tale from the *Sketch Book,* "Rip Van Winkle." Although little formal criticism greeted the arrival of the story specifically, the *Sketch Book* became wildly popular and widely reviewed both in the United States and in England. It was the first book by an American writer to become popular outside the United States, and helped establish American writing as a serious and respectable literature. In 1864, "The Legend of Sleepy Hollow" was published as a separate illustrated volume for the first time, and there have been dozens of editions since. Today, most of Irving's work has been largely forgotten, but the characters of Ichabod Crane and the Headless Horseman have lived on as part of American folklore.

Author Biography

Considering that Irving's best-known fiction takes place in the countryside of rural upstate New York, it is perhaps surprising that he spent most of the first thirty-two years of his life in New York City, where he was born on April 3, 1783. He was the eleventh child of immigrant parents, and remained close to his family all his life. Irving's family had money and some influence in New York, and he received a solid education and then studied the law. He was only a mediocre student, and would probably not have made a good lawyer. Instead, he turned to a somewhat leisurely life as a man of letters, attending parties and the theatre, traveling around the state, and writing humorous newspaper pieces under a false name, Jonathan Oldstyle, Gent.

In 1807, Irving was part of a group that collaborated on a humorous periodical called *Salmagundi,* poking fun at the manners and customs of the day, describing the fashions, theatre and arts in wicked detail. The style of the pieces echoed essays written by the English writer Joseph Addison, but with determinedly American subjects. There were no important American literary influences for Irving to follow; the United States was still young enough that its artists had to look to Europe for their models. His first book was *A History of New York from the Beginning of the World to the End of the Dutch Dynasty* (1809), satirizing Dutch customs and manners, and also the pretentious writing style of historians.

He sailed to Europe in 1815, and lived there for the next seventeen years, finding acclaim as a writer and as a diplomat. His most enduring book, *The Sketch Book,* from which "The Legend of Sleepy Hollow" and "Rip Van Winkle" are taken, was published in America beginning in 1819, and in England in 1820. It was the first book by an American writer to reach a wide international audience, and proved to the world that America had subjects and themes that were of interest to Europeans. Irving wrote many more books, but never wrote as well again as he had in the *Sketch Book.*

Back in his homeland, he traveled across the plains of the western frontier, and finally bought a large rural property in Sleepy Hollow, a valley near Tarrytown, New York, where he entertained the many people who wanted to meet the famous writer. He died on November 28, 1859, at the age of 76—a long life for the nineteenth century. He is buried in the Sleepy Hollow cemetery. Although in his own lifetime Irving was considered the most important writer America had ever produced, almost none of his books are read today. Only a few of his short stories live on, still loved for their vivid descriptions and humor.

Plot Summary

The story opens with a long descriptive passage offered in the first person by the narrator, who is revealed at the end of the story to be a man in a tavern who told the story to "D. K." Irving's contemporaries, and readers of the entire *Sketch Book,* know that "D. K." is Diedrich Knickerbocker, the fictional author of an earlier book of Irving's. The narrator describes the story's setting, creating images of a quaint, cozy Dutch village, "one of the quietest places in the whole world," in a "remote period of American history" that seemed long-ago even to Irving's original readers. The village is not just far away and long ago; it is a magical place, "under the sway of some witching power, that holds a spell over the minds of the good people, causing them to walk in a continual reverie."

In this land lives Ichabod Crane, a schoolteacher and singing instructor who comes from Connecticut. His last name suits him. He is tall, lanky and sharp-featured, with clothes too small and ears too big. Crane is a serious and strict teacher, but liked well enough by his students and their families. He has apparently no real friends in the community, but is welcome as he passes from house to house eating whatever he can help himself to in exchange for doing light chores and entertaining the housewives with his stories and gossip. He is much admired for his intelligence, for, unlike the rest of the village, he has "read several books quite through," and he is especially interested in tales of witchcraft and magic. Several local tales feature the ghost of a Hessian trooper, who was killed by a cannonball and who rides through the countryside each night looking for his missing head.

One of Crane's singing students, Katrina Van Tassel, has caught his eye, and he dreams of marrying her. Katrina is eighteen years old, plump and ripe, and "a little of a coquette." Crane desires her not because of her beauty or her personality, but because her father is wealthy and there is always wonderful food at the Van Tassel home. He fills his thoughts with images of roast pigs and pies and sausages, and imagines selling off the Van Tassel land to buy a homestead in the wilderness where he and Katrina "with a whole family of children" could go in a covered wagon. So Crane begins to court Katrina.

Because she is beautiful and wealthy, Katrina has other suitors. Chief among them is Brom Bones, a man who is everything Ichabod Crane is not: strong, rugged, handsome, humorous and clever. Katrina seems content to be courted by two men, and does not discourage either man's attentions. Brom's natural instinct is to fight with Crane, but since Crane will not fight Brom resorts to playing a series of practical jokes on Crane instead.

One evening, Mr. Van Tassel hosts a big party for everyone in the village. Crane dresses up in his finest and makes himself look as handsome as he can. He is so awestruck by the tremendous food-laden tables at the party that he decides to ask

Katrina for her hand. After an evening of swapping ghost stories with his neighbors, he approaches his intended bride. Although the discussion is not recorded, a few minutes later he leaves the house "with an air quite desolate and chop-fallen." Feeling dismal, he begins the long ride home alone. Remembering all the ghost stories he has heard and told that evening, he gets more and more nervous.

Suddenly, he sees a large shadowy figure on the road ahead. It appears to be a headless man riding a horse, and Crane can just make out the shape of a head resting on the pommel of the saddle. Terrified, he races away, chased by the headless horseman. He is unable to escape. The last thing he remembers is the sight of the rider about to throw the head at him; struck by the flying object, he is knocked unconscious to the ground.

The next morning Crane does not come to school, and he is never seen in the village again. A search party finds his hat and a bundle of his possessions, and nearby on the ground a smashed pumpkin. Brom Bones marries Katrina, and for the rest of his life gives a knowing look and a laugh when the mysterious disappearance of his rival is mentioned. Though some in the village may suspect that Brom was responsible for Crane's disappearance, most of the women maintain that Crane was carried away by the headless horseman. Crane himself has become the subject of the kind of ghost story he so loved to tell.

Characters

Brom Bones

See Abraham Van Brunt

Ichabod Crane

Ichabod Crane, the protagonist, is a stern schoolteacher and singing instructor who has come to Sleepy Hollow, New York, from Connecticut. He is lanky and sharp-featured, awkward and somewhat clumsy, but more educated and sophisticated than the native villagers. He is quite fond of food, and is well fed by the neighboring housewives, who share his delight in telling and re-telling ghost stories. When he sets his sights on marrying Katrina Van Tassel, it is not because of any feeling he has for her, but because her father is wealthy and Crane admires the food that is always displayed in the Van Tassel home. Katrina refuses him, however, preferring the manly and strong Brom Bones. In his disappointment Crane allows his imagination to run away with him. He is tricked by Brom into believing that he is being chased through the night by a headless horseman. In the morning he is gone, having left town without saying good-bye.

Media Adaptations

- "The Legend of Sleepy Hollow" has been recorded by Donada Peters as part of a five-hour set of audiotapes titled *Rip Van Winkle and Other Stories*. The set is distributed by Books on Tape, Inc. The story is also available on audiocassette as a musical dramatization that has received excellent reviews. Produced by Reed Publishing USA in 1993, it is part of the Carousel Classics collection.

- The story is also available on videocassette. *Tales of Washington Irving* (1987) is a videocassette release of animated films made in 1970. Distributed by MGM/UA Home Video, the 48-minute tape contains "The Legend of Sleepy Hollow" and "Rip Van Winkle", and features the voice talents of Mel Blanc and other familiar stars. Another videotape, *The Legend of Sleepy Hollow by Washington Irving,* uses human actors and sets the story in a recreated early American-Dutch settlement. Published by Guidance Associates, it is designed to motivate students to read the story.

- Among the many film versions, two deserve special note. *Shelley Duvall's Tall Tales and Legends: The Legend of Sleepy Hollow* is a 52-minute film starring Ed Begley, Jr., and is distributed by Trimark. Scheduled for a November 1999 cinema release is a major motion picture, *Sleepy Hollow,* directed by Tim Burton and starring Johnny Depp as Ichabod Crane.

Abraham Van Brunt

Brom Bones is Crane's chief rival for Katrina's affections, and is in every way Crane's opposite. He is large, strong, rough, humorous, and good-natured, as well-known for his skill as a horseman as Crane is for his education. When he sees that

Crane is paying attention to Katrina, Brom begins a series of practical jokes to humiliate him. Finally, he disguises himself as the headless horseman and chases the impressionable Crane through the darkness. When Crane leaves town, Bones marries Katrina.

Baltus Van Tassel

Old Baltus Van Tassel is a veteran of the American Revolution, and the patriarch of a wealthy Dutch farming family. He owns a large, well-kept home and barn, with livestock and fertile fields. Van Tassel is a warm and generous neighbor and an indulgent father. He does not interfere in his daughter's dalliances with the local young men.

Katrina Van Tassel

Katrina is the eighteen-year-old daughter of Baltus Van Tassel and his wife. She is beautifully plump and rosy-cheeked, and always dresses to enhance and emphasize her attractiveness. She is flattered by the attentions of the young men, and does nothing to encourage or discourage Ichabod Crane and Brom Bones from flirting with her. But when Crane presses for a commitment, she sends him away, and soon after marries Brom.

Themes

City versus Country

One of the great themes of American literature and American folklore is the clash between the city and the country, between civilization and the wilderness.

Topics for Further Study

- Find a few of the many illustrated versions of "The Legend of Sleepy Hollow" in the children's section of the library, or some of the video or filmstrip versions. Compare the pictures of Ichabod Crane in these versions with Irving's descriptions in the text. How precisely does

Irving describe Crane? How closely do the pictures match your own vision of Crane's appearance?

- Find a copy of "The Castle of Indolence," a poem from 1748 written by the Scottish poet James Thomson. Why might Irving attached four lines of this poem to his own story? What do the two pieces have in common?

- Research the status of African Americans in New York during the end of the eighteenth century. Analyze Irving's casual disrespect for the "Negro" characters in his story in terms of how his contemporary readers would have responded to it, and in terms of how modern readers might respond.

- Closely examine the passages in which Irving describes food in lingering detail. Based on the modern food pyramid, how healthy was the diet of wealthy Dutch farmers in the late 1800s?

As the theme is played out in literature around the world, it carries one of two interpretations: either the city is seen as beautiful, civilized, rich, clean and safe, and the country is ugly, dirty and dangerous, or else the city is dirty and dangerous, populated by swindlers who love nothing better than tricking the kind, gentle people from the beautiful country. American folklore from the nineteenth century tends to favor the second view. Settlers were proud of their wilderness, and excited by it, and their stories celebrated the skills and qualities one needed to survive on the frontier. The heroes from this period—Daniel Boone, Mike Fink, Paul Bunyan, John Henry, the Swamp Angel—are rugged, strong and clever. When supposedly educated city slickers venture into the countryside, they are outsmarted by these heroes every time.

Ichabod Crane, a native of Connecticut, is a typical scholar who wishes he were an outdoorsman. Irving points out that there are two types of men who come out of Connecticut, "pioneers for the mind as well as for the forest," who become "frontier woodmen and country schoolmasters." Crane is not completely out of place in the forest—he is able to help with the "lighter labors" on the farm— but thinks of himself and is considered by others "a kind of idle gentleman-like personage, of vastly superior taste and accomplishments to the rough country swains." On Sunday afternoons, while he strolls about with the young ladies of the village, "the more bashful country bumpkins h[a]ng sheepishly back, envying his superior elegance and address."

Brom Bones, Crane's most formidable competitor for the hand of Katrina, is as unlike Crane as he could be, "burly, roaring, roistering." Where Crane is "esteemed by the women as a man of great erudition," Brom is "the hero of the country round, which rang with his feats of strength and hardihood." Crane is "tall, but exceedingly lank, with narrow shoulders," while Brom is "broad-shouldered" and has a "Herculean frame." Crane courts Katrina "in a quiet and gently insinuating manner," while Brom's "amorous toyings" are "something like the gentle caresses and endearments of a bear."

Irving sets up a confrontation between these two opposites, and any reader of American folklore knows how it will turn out. Crane's education is no match for Brom's native wit, his scrawny body and awkward riding are no match for Brom's strength and skill, and the woman chooses the rough and strong man over the refined and delicate one. Neither man is particularly unlikable, but in America, a young country with frontier to be tamed, the values of the country win out over those of the city.

Creativity and Imagination

"The Legend of Sleepy Hollow" is a story about stories and story-tellers, and a lesson in keeping the line clear between fiction and reality. The title is significant. Irving identifies this as a legend, a type of story that may be loosely based on truth but is clearly fiction, that may feature the supernatural, that is handed down by a people and that reflects the national character of that people.

This quality is captured in "The Legend of

Sleepy Hollow" as the narrator reminds the reader again and again of the special nature of the valley where the story takes place. The name of the valley is no accident, for "a drowsy dreamy influence seems to hang over the land, and to pervade the very atmosphere." The place "holds a spell over the minds of the good people, causing them to walk in a continual reverie." Ichabod Crane is not immune to the influence, for even outsiders, "however wide awake they may have been before they entered that sleepy region," are sure to "inhale the witching atmosphere of the air, and begin to grow imaginative."

One function of imagination and story-telling is to bind a community together, as seen in the party scene. Most of the stories told are unverifiable and untrue: "Just sufficient time had elapsed to enable each story-teller to dress up his tale with a little becoming fiction, and, in the indistinctness of his recollection, to make himself the hero of every exploit." The exaggeration is just part of the fun, and so long as everyone understands this there is no harm.

Crane, however, does not understand the limits of imagination. His dreams are too grand; he tries to make them reality but he can never live up to them. When he sees the bounty at the Van Tassel home, he dreams "in his devouring mind's eye" of "every roasting-pig running about with a pudding in his belly" and every turkey and duck and pigeon becoming a meal for him. When he looks over the Van Tassel land, "his imagination expanded with the idea, how they might be readily turned into cash." And when he looks into the mirror as he prepares for the party, he sees a cavalier, where the narrator sees only a "grasshopper." No wonder Crane is bold enough to ask for Katrina's hand, and no wonder he is surprised when she refuses him.

This lack of discernment is Crane's downfall. Because he imagines himself to be a "knight-errant in quest of adventures," he humiliates himself in front of Katrina. Because he does not understand that the story of the headless horseman is just a story, he is easy prey for Brom. If only he were as wise as the story-teller in Knickerbocker's postscript, who says of his own story, "Faith sir . . . I don't believe one half of it myself."

Style

Narration/Narrative/Narrator

There is an almost dizzying number of levels of narration and narrators in "The Legend of Sleepy Hollow": a) Washington Irving is the author of *The Sketch Book of Geoffrey Crayon, Gent.* ; b) Geoffrey Crayon is the fictional author of the volume, the one responsible for collection or creating the stories and sketches; c) Diedrich Knickerbocker is the character who supposedly wrote down "The Legend of Sleepy Hollow," and in whose hand the postscript was "found," presumably by Crayon; d) the legend was told to Knickerbocker by a "pleasant, shabby, gentlemanly old fellow"; e) within the legend, the characters tell stories that they have heard or read, many of them concerning "a figure on horseback without a head." Ichabod Crane, then, is a man who is frightened by a story within a story within a story within a story.

The narrators are not only numerous, but also unreliable. Knickerbocker claims that he has repeated the legend "almost in the precise words in which I heard it related"—a ridiculous claim considering the length of the story, the amount of description, and the fact that he heard it only once. The "gentlemanly old fellow" makes a great pretense in the beginning of his narration of telling the truth, pointing out that he has heard an explanation for the name "Tarry Town," but he will not "vouch for the fact, but merely advert to it, for the sake of being precise and accurate." By the end, however, he admits that the legend might be a bit extravagant, and says, "I don't believe one half of it myself."

The inhabitants of Sleepy Hollow are subject to fits of imagination, "they are given to all kinds of marvelous beliefs," and they enjoy gatherings at which each story-teller is encouraged "to dress up his tale with a little becoming fiction, and, in the indistinction of his recollection, to make himself the hero of every exploit." When the men are not telling stories of how they won the war single-handedly, they are telling "tales of ghosts and apparitions," and finding the stories delightfully frightening. As narrators, they are as unreliable as Knickerbocker and his acquaintance.

The effect of all these unreliable narrators is to distance the reader from the action and from the characters. If nothing can be believed, empathy cannot develop, and the reader forms no strong feelings about Crane, either positive or negative. As a psychological study, "The Legend of Sleepy Hollow" falls short, because the reader never gets close enough to the characters to look inside their minds. Cardboard characters move through a humorous situation, and although there is some trickery afoot, no one really gets hurt. This emotional distance, created by the multiple levels of narration, focuses readers' attention on the humor, and it is the humor that has made "The Legend of

Sleepy Hollow" an American favorite for almost two hundred years.

Imagery

One of the most striking features of the story is the long passages of rich descriptive detail. The narrator opens with a long reverie on the dreaminess of the landscape, but when the story shifts its focus to Crane and his thoughts, the description becomes more vivid. When Crane walks home in the evening, for example, the narrator lists every creature that frightens him: the whip-poor-will, the tree-toad, the screech-owl, the fire-flies, the beetle. When he looks over the Van Tassel barn, "bursting forth with the treasures of the farm," Crane's gaze — and the reader's— lingers over every swallow, martin, pigeon, pig, goose, duck, turkey, guinea-fowl and rooster.

When he sees a farm animal, Crane imagines it as food, and the list of farm creatures is followed immediately by a longer list of the dishes they might yield. "In his devouring mind's eye" Crane sees the pigs roasted, the pigeons "snugly put to bed in a comfortable pie," the ducks "pairing cozily in dishes, like snug married couples, with a decent competency of onion sauce." Inside the Van Tassel home, Crane cannot keep his eyes still as he admires the tools, the furniture, and most importantly the fruits of the earth: "In one corner stood a huge bag of wool ready to be spun; in another, a quantity of linsey-woolsey just from the loom; ears of Indian corn, and strings of dried apples and peaches, hung in gay festoons along the wall, mingled with the gaud of red peppers." Where other men are attracted to Katrina because of her beauty, Crane sees her only as a stepping stone to "the treasures of jolly autumn."

William Hedges observes that "the method of this story is to heap up images of abundance and contrast Sleepy Hollow's amplitude with the meagreness of Ichabod Crane's body and spirit." Mary Weatherspoon Bowden refers to the same images of "glorious autumn days and autumn harvests, to food, food, and more food, to buxom lasses and merriment and pranks" when she concludes that the legend is "a celebration of the bounty of the United States."

For Americans at the beginning of the nineteenth century, the United States was still the land of plenty, a country of endless resources. This was a source of pride for Irving and his American readers, and a subject of fascination and wonder for his British readers, whose national wilderness had been tamed centuries before. Irving uses lush imagery precisely for its lushness, to demonstrate and celebrate the endless resources of a new, unproven nation.

The Dutch in New York

In its earliest days as an outpost for Europeans, New York was settled by the Dutch, or people from the Kingdom of the Netherlands. Henry Hudson, referred to in "The Legend of Sleepy Hollow" as "Master Hendrick Hudson," sailed in 1609 from present-day New York City to Albany up what the Dutch called the Tappan Zee, and what is now called the Hudson River; the Tappan Zee Bridge in New York City commemorates this today. Hudson was British by birth, but was working for the Dutch East India Company, and after his explorations the Netherlands claimed what is now New York as its own territory. The first Dutch settlers arrived at present-day New York City in 1624. Although the territory eventually came under British and then American control, the Dutch people were still numerous and influential throughout New York in Irving's day.

Compare & Contrast

- **1810:** Irving's home town, New York City, is a major metropolitan center with a population of 80,000. The population of the United States is 7,239,881.

1990: The population of New York City is 7,322,564.

- **1810s:** Women's bodies are thought to be attractive if they are, like, Katrina Van Tassel's, "plump as a partridge." Many women think it is vulgar to be thin enough that the shape of their bones is revealed.

  1990s: Women are expected to be thin. Defined cheekbones are a mark of beauty.

- **1810s:** Few people in a rural village are educated enough to teach school. Most people are not able to read and write. Therefore, teachers come from outside, often from the cities.

  1990s: Adults who cannot read or write have great difficulties managing daily life.

- **1810s:** Veterans of the American Revolution are still alive, and enjoy telling true and exaggerated war stories at social occasions.

  1990s: Veterans of the Korean and Vietnam conflicts tend to keep quiet about their experiences.

As with any ethnic group, stereotypes of the Dutch were abundant. They were said to be jolly, prosperous, well-fed, and foolish. Irving had poked fun at Dutchmen in *A History of New York from the Beginning of the World to the End of the Dutch Dynasty*, whose fictional author was Diedrich Knickerbocker. Knickerbocker is supposedly the source of this story as well, and the stereotypes are used to comic effect in the characters of Baltus Van Tassel, his daughter Katrina, and their superstitious and somewhat pompous neighbors. It should be said that there were also widespread stereotypical notions about Yankees, or people of Anglo-Saxon descent, who were considered—like Ichabod Crane — to be vain, overeducated, sophisticated and lacking in common sense.

Irving made use of the folklore about Dutch people, and in a minor way contributed to it. When he created the character of Diedrich Knickerbocker, he made up the name "Knickerbocker" to sound funny and at the same time come close enough to a genuine Dutch name to be believable. With Irving's growing popularity, people began to associate the last name with the people. Dutch people were referred to as "knickerbockers," and later the baggy pants gathered below the knee that the men wore came to be known as "knickerbockers" and then "knickers." Knickers fell out of fashion after the 1930s, but the name is still used by the professional basketball team the Knickerbockers, or the New York Knicks.

The New American Fiction

Irving was alive and writing at the moment in American literary history when a true national literature was being called for and created. Previously, the writing coming out of the colonies and then out of the new nation was primarily religious or historical, and was scarcely different from the same kinds of writing coming out of Europe. Ichabod Crane's own favorite writer, Cotton Mather (1663-1728), was a preacher and a political writer of rational, stern treatises on subjects of the day. His books about witchcraft grew out of the Salem witchcraft trials, and they were neither imaginative, nor intended to entertain or to express the writer's experiences or emotions. Instead, in *The History of New England Witchcraft*, which Daniel Hoffman has identified as *Magnalia Christi Americana* (1702), Mather presented case histories of what he believed to be actual and Satanic events, for the purpose of informing his readers and arguing against the witch trials.

By the end of the eighteenth century, there was a demand for American characters and American themes, and plays filling this need had already begun to appear. The popularity of novels imported from England led to the beginnings of the American novel, and to serious discussions about what kinds of literature would best reflect the values of a democratic society. Irving was among the first American writers who had both the talent and the will to write American fiction, but he had no American models.

The Sketch Book, written in England, contains

more than thirty sketches or stories, and nearly all of them have to do with English life and English characters. "The Legend of Sleepy Hollow" was unusual, though not unique, in being set in the United States. To create the story, Irving borrowed heavily from the German legends of Ruebezahl from the *Volksmaerchen der Deutschen,* transporting the basic action and characters to Upstate New York. It was a beginning. The *Sketch Book* became the first book by an American to sell well in England, proving that it could be done.

Historians and critics have debated for over a century whether Irving invented the short story when he wrote "The Legend of Sleepy Hollow" and "Rip Van Winkle." Some have argued that the two are not actually stories at all, but merely tales. Whether he was a creator or an adapter, a writer of stories or of tales, Irving expanded the possibilities of American writing, and helped make possible the explosion of new forms and idioms that would come along at the middle of the nineteenth century.

Critical Overview

Most early readers of *The Sketch Book* praised the volume for its humor and its graceful descriptive writing, but did not single out "The Legend of Sleepy Hollow" for special attention. Francis Jeffrey, in an 1820 review in *Edinburgh Review,* did note that the legend, along with "Rip Van Winkle," was among only five or six pieces in the collection of thirty-five that relates "to subjects at all connected with America. . . . The rest relate entirely to England." But other than pointing out its existence, he had nothing to say about the story. Jeffrey was clearly delighted with the collection, and astonished that Irving was able to produce it: "It is the work of an American, entirely bred and trained in that country. . . . Now, the most remarkable thing in a work so circumstanced certainly is, that it should be written throughout with the greatest care and accuracy, and worked up to great purity and beauty of diction."

More recently, critics have attempted to delineate just what is American about Irving's fiction. Terence Martin, writing for *American Literature* in 1959, focuses his attention on the newness of the United States as a nation during Irving's career, and the American tendency at the time to equate "the imaginative and the childish." Irving's struggling to control his appetite and to use imagination properly can be seen as mirroring the struggles of the new society to behave maturely. He concludes, "for Irving there is no place, or a very limited place, for the hero of the imagination in the culture of early America." In *The Comic Imagination in American Literature* (1973), Lewis Leary traces the influence Irving's work had on American humor, and claims that in "The Legend of Sleepy Hollow" and other early tales, Irving "opened doors which gave access to native varieties of the comic spirit."

Around the middle of the twentieth century, attention was turned toward finding the sources Irving used in crafting his tales. The most important work was done by Henry A. Pochmann in 1930. In articles in *Studies in Philology* and *PMLA [Publications of the Modern Language Association]*, Pochmann demonstrated that Irving had translated and adapted German stories to create "The Legend of Sleepy Hollow" and other tales. In a 1953 article in *PMLA*, Daniel G. Hoffman explored Irving's use of American folkloric sources, finding that Irving used great "originality in interpreting American themes," and he developed his ideas further in his 1961 book, *Form and Fable in American Fiction*.

In the last quarter century, some critics have examined the story from a feminist perspective, to examine what the story reveals about Irving's ideas about the role of women. In her 1975 book *The Lay of the Land*, Annette Kolodny describes Sleepy Hollow as a feminine pastoral setting. She sees Ichabod Crane as a male aggressor who threatens this community and therefore must be driven away.

In 1993, Laura Plummer and Michael Nelson again find that Crane is "an intrusive male who threatens the stability of a decidedly feminine place," as they explain in an article in *Studies in Short Fiction*. They describe the story as a conflict between male and female forms of storytelling, and point out its "misogynistic bent."

Other critics have seen Crane as threatening, but in different ways. Writing for *American Imago* in 1981, Edward F. Pajak explains how the legend is a variation of the myth of Narcissus, and describes Crane's "poorly integrated identity." Crane's attraction to Katrina and her father masks his unconscious attraction to Brom Bones, and he can find resolution only by "a rejection of the world." For Albert J. von Frank, Crane is more than paranoid and regressed. He finds in a 1987 article in *Studies in American Fiction* that "Irving' s genial reputation largely obscures the evil that Ichabod represents." Crane's envy, avarice, sloth and gluttony, among other sins, threaten the community with "moral taint and eventual destruction," making it necessary to drive him from the village.

Sources

Bowden, Mary Weatherspoon. *Washington Irving,* Boston: Twayne, 1981, p. 72.

Giamatti, A. Bartlett. *The Earthly Paradise and the Renaissance Epic,* Princeton, N.J.: Princeton University Press, 1966, pp. 3, 6, 34, 126-27.

Hedges, William L. *Washington Irving: An American Study, 1802-1832,* Baltimore: Johns Hopkins Press, 1965, p. 142.

Hoffman, Daniel G. *Form and Fable in American Fiction,* New York: Oxford University Press, 1961.

_____. "Irving's Use of American Folklore in 'The Legend of Sleepy Hollow,'" in *PMLA,* Vol. 68, June, 1953, pp. 425-435.

Jeffrey, Francis. Review of *The Sketch Book,* in *Edinburgh Review,* Vol. 34, August, 1820, pp. 160-76.

Kolodny, Annette. *The Lay of the Land: Metaphor as Experience and History in American Life and Letters,* Chapel Hill: University of North Carolina Press, 1975, pp. 68-70.

Leary, Lewis. "Washington Irving and the Comic Imagination," in *The Comic Imagination in American Literature,* ed. Louis D. Rubin. New Brunswick: Rutgers University Press, 1973, pp. 63-76.

Martin, Terence. "Rip, Ichabod, and the American

Imagination," in *American Literature,* Vol. 31, May, 1959, pp. 137-149.

Pataj, Edward F. "Washington Irving's Ichabod Crane: American Narcissus," in *American Imago,* Vol. 38, Spring, 1981, pp. 127-35.

Plummer, Laura, and Michael Nelson. "'Girls Can Take Care of Themselves'; Gender and Storytelling in Washington Irving's 'The Legend of Sleepy Hollow,'" in *Studies in Short Fiction,* Vol. 30, 1993, pp. 175-84.

Pochmann, Henry A. "Irving's German Tour and Its Influence on His Tales," in *PMLA,* Vol. 45, December, 1930, pp. 1150-87.

_____. "Irving's German Sources in *The Sketch Book,"* in *Studies in Philology,* Vol. 27, July, 1930, pp. 477-507.

Theocritus. "Idyll VII," in *The Greek Bucolic Poets,* translated by J. E. Edmonds, Cambridge, Mass.: Loeb Library, 1938, lines 135-46.

von Frank, Albert J. "The Man That Corrupted Sleepy Hollow," in *Studies in American Fiction,* Vol. 15, No. 2, 1987, pp. 129-143.

Further Reading

Aderman, Ralph M., ed. *Critical Essays on Washington Irving,* Boston: G. K. Hall, 1990.

> A survey of Irving criticism, with a selection of early nineteenth-century reviews as well as twentieth-century scholarly articles.

Bowden, Edwin T. *Washington Irving: Bibliography,* Boston: Twayne, 1989.

> Volume 30 in *The Complete Works of Washington Irving,* this is the most complete and up-to-date bibliography available.

Bowden, Mary Weatherspoon. *Washington Irving,* Boston: Twayne, 1981.

> The best introduction for the general reader, dealing chronologically with each of Irving's major works.

Hedges, William L. *Washington Irving: An American Study, 1802-1832,* Baltimore: Johns Hopkins Press, 1965.

> Insightful literary analysis of Irving's major works, which Hedges believes are those written before his return to the United States.

Tuttleton, James W., ed. *Washington Irving: The Critical Reaction,* New York: AMS Press, 1993.

Sixteen critical essays about Irving's work. Three of the essays treat "Sleepy Hollow" directly, and two others help establish the context for the early work, including *The Sketch Book*.

Wagenknecht, Edward. *Washington Irving: Moderation Displayed,* New York: Oxford University Press, 1962.

An accessible biography and critical overview, emphasizing Irving's stature during his own lifetime as the United States' most significant writer.

CPSIA information can be obtained
at www.ICGtesting.com
Printed in the USA
BVHW081520080419
544915BV00015B/1337/P